THE AUTISM LIFE

A Mom's Perspective

Jessica Eggleston

CONTENTS

For my kids.

LET'S START AT THE VERY BEGINNING

How did we get here? If you've been down this road, you know sometimes it can be pretty complicated. Sometimes disorders are really obvious; sometimes they aren't, and then of course, you don't know what you don't know. I'm not an expert in disorders (though I feel like one after years of learning!). I'm just a mom who's been through it. Everyone's journey to a diagnosis looks different, but maybe you will see a little of your story in mine.

When my son, who I will refer to as E, was a baby, he didn't really talk. At age 1, he said so few words his doctor told me I should take him to a speech therapist, but it was so alarming, the way they told me, I got a second opinion. Another doctor told me it wasn't anything to worry about because he was so loving and social and that when he did start talking, I'd be wishing for the silence. Other people also told me they thought it wasn't anything to worry about, their kid was quiet at first too, and I decided not to take him at age 1 to speech therapy. He started to speak a few more words, and at his 15 month appointment, I saw a different doctor. That doctor didn't know why the other doctor would have told me to get speech therapy, so I felt better even though I was still afraid I was missing something. I knew the worry was that silence = autism but my son was friendly, looked people in the eye, and didn't seem to exhibit other signs so everyone that knew this was a concern told me he was fine, and I listened.

When E was 18 months old, he already recognized all the letters of the alphabet and was clearly a smart kid, though still quiet. He had a long attention span, especially for his age, if he was doing something he really loved. He was skilled at doing puzzles in an interesting way: instead of trial and error, he would study the board, look at the pieces, then pick up the shape and put it exactly in the right spot. He built tall towers, taller than he should have been able to for his age according to all the benchmark charts. Regarding language, he would test out a word, say it, and then never say it again, but he could follow multi-step directions. All of these things, except for the quietness, pointed to giftedness, not something wrong- at least as far as we understood it. One day my husband and I walked into his room and found him playing with this elaborate construction he had made, with a teapot lid spinning on the top. I distinctly remember thinking, as I saw him sitting there, "Oh my God, he's autistic." But again, I never followed up because so many people I trusted me he couldn't possibly be autistic. In retrospect I should have trusted my gut but I didn't. As time went on, I knew I needed answers. I knew something was wrong, but I didn't know what.

When my son was very little, he didn't want to play with Play-Doh, play in the dirt, color, paint, or anything of that nature. I chalked it up variously to him being a boy, or his age, or just personality, as did everyone I talked to. When he was a little older he wouldn't really play with other kids. He couldn't instinctively pick up the rules of a game where other little kids would just somehow know what to do (or not care, they'd just jump in.) He'd stand and watch to be sure what to do, or just play by himself.

When he started at school, a private school/home school hybrid, there were other things that starting appearing. He would use both hands equally. His handwriting was bad. He still had no interest in coloring, his work was sloppy, he had a hard time following directions. Now I can rattle off all the terms involved here: not crossing midline, poor gross and fine motor skills, and so on, but all I knew was he wasn't doing normal kid stuff.

In the midst of all this, he was decoding words by 3, and at age 6, was measured as reading at a middle school level and that's because they stopped measuring at the therapist's office because he flew through every decoding test. Basically he could read any word outloud, but knowing meaning/application was another matter. He had an amazing ability to memorize, wanted to please, knew in his head what he was supposed to do, but would have, and still does have, a hard time executing.

So, here was my boy, who I knew was smart, but who was overly literal, lacking in empathy, crying about random things, who couldn't carry on a conversation because he doesn't pick up on social cues and would burst out with non-sequiturs all the time, would fling himself out of his chair during homeschool, chewed on his fingers, couldn't seem to connect what I was saying to him with what he was supposed to be doing, I could literally point to the exact spot where he was supposed to fill something in on a worksheet and he'd put it in the wrong place, he had a hard time making eye contact with people... and I had no idea why any of these things were happening. His earliest teachers thought he'd grow out of it.

Then came the fateful day. E was in first grade working on a writing assignment. He kept writing a word incorrectly, recognizing it as wrong, erasing it, rewriting it the same wrong way, erasing it, to the point where he had destroyed the paper, and crying. It was like he was stuck in a loop.

I had been in communication with all his teachers about these things, but because he was so young none of it seemed like a red flag until first grade. His teacher told me about that event, along with some other behaviors she had noticed and she suggested I get him checked out for sensory processing issues.

Being who I am, I did a ton of research on what that was, and got my dad, who worked in the health care world, on the job of finding the best place to go for an evaluation. Reading about sensory processing disorder seemed like the authors had been spying on my life. When I got him in to an occupational therapist, the evaluation revealed the answers I had been desperately seeking, or so I thought.

He had a slew of issues that went along with the now-official diagnosis of sensory processing disorder: not crossing midline which affected basically everything, problems with his vestibular and proprioceptive sense, poor fine motor control, and other things. The OT suggested an audiologist visit, which revealed a problem with binaural integration. Basically, if there are multiple sounds going on, his brain shuts them all out. The audiologist suggested a visual processing assessment. That revealed severe problems with tracking and binocular vision. Basically his eyes were skipping all over the page when reading, while at the same time he was basically seeing double, and his eyes were working overtime to converge.

One of the doctors explained to me that E throwing himself out of his chair all the time was like a power surge. Because his brain and body weren't communicating correctly, he would get all this sensory input and it wasn't being sorted right, but it had to go somewhere, hence these bursts. These diagnoses explained, for example, why I could point to the exact spot on a page where he should put his pencil and he couldn't do it, or why his letters would be floating in space or below the line, or illegible, or some combination thereof.

The visual doctor also told me that E was clearly gifted and had been compensating in an amazing way all this time, to be able to decode as well and as fast as he can when his eyes are jumping all over the place and seeing double. That was also what had stumped all of us involved in his education- he was clearly smart; that was never the problem. After a year and a half of therapy and seeing some of these issues be resolved, there was still something off.

He'd gotten a lot better with his therapy but there were some things that just set off flags to me. He still struggled socially and with looking people in the eye. Didn't want people in his personal space, wouldn't voluntarily say "I love you." I discovered he'd been ripping paper out of books and chewing on it. I asked his occupational therapist about it, she said talk to the pediatrician, the pediatrician said, "You need to take him to a psychologist." It turned out that initial diagnosis from early 2016 was only part of the story, just symptoms of a greater problem. In summer of 2017 he received a diagnosis of autism, anxiety, ADHD, multiple learning disabilities, and OCD tendencies. This sent us back to therapy and medication, and there has been dramatic improvement. While he will always be autistic, we are fighting like hell to overcome as much as we can.

HISTORY OF AUTISM

Autism is a nebulous diagnosis. A common phrase in this world is, "If you've met one person with autism, you've met one person with autism." There are many reasons for this. Here's a quick history. Autism was only barely discussed as its own diagnosis in the early-mid 20th century; prior to that it was seen as a particular manifestation or symptom of schizophrenia or seen as unimportant to diagnose because the treatment was all the same: institutionalization. The definition, such as it was back then, was also limited to extreme cases-the non-verbal, violent, impulsive, danger-to-self-and-others cases. Because it was hard to define, the powers that be weren't interested. It took lots of personally invested powerful people with money to get a move on with investigating this disorder.

Another reason why this diagnosis is nebulous is because there was a debate on whether autism and Asperger's were different things. Add on top of that that families were loathe to take their children in because historically, either they'd lose their kids, be blamed for causing the autism by being "refrigerator mothers," or have their kids treated as lab rats. (Not an exaggeration- in the mid-late 20th century autistic kids were used in experiments with LSD, without consent by any family member.)

Even ABA therapy, which is the norm for treatment now, has its roots in controversy as it was developed from delivering electric shock therapy and other "treatments" horrifying by any standard, much less our modern one. The rush to blame parents or some other entity, rather than just accept that this is just a thing that happens, still pervades in an unhelpful manner. Today it manifests in the dangerous, disproven lies of vaccinations as the cause and even now there is stigma rooted in lack of knowledge on what autism means. And all the while, there was debate over whether Asperger's and autism were different things.

In 2013, the DSM-5, the manual used to diagnose mental disorders, eliminated Asperger's as a discrete diagnosis and included those symptoms in the much broader diagnosis of Autism Spectrum Disorder, or ASD. (Side note: Asperger was a straight-up Nazi.) Another reason for rising numbers of autism diagnoses are doctors will diagnose it even if it's not exactly autism because it opens doors to services and financial aid and insurance payments that aren't there if you just have a processing issue, for example. They're doing you a solid in many cases.

No one knows what causes autism, but it's not vaccines. The link between MMR and autism was literally invented out of whole-cloth by a total charlatan named Andrew Wakefield. He made up his test results and presented a link that he invented as fact because he wanted to patent his own vaccine, so he had a selfish financial stake in trying to discredit this successful, harmless vaccine. Even though he was fully discredited and there was no evidence at all that the MMR vaccine caused autism, it was too late. People believed his lies. (Have I mentioned that he MADE IT UP?)

Jenny McCarthyism was sweeping the nation. (I wish I had invented that term, but alas, I did not.) The scientific, medical, and judicial systems have investigated this idea and found that there is no link. A recent study even showed a higher rate of autism in unvaccinated children! But there is still a growing, influential movement that holds to this idea, sharing memes and scaremongering articles with a veneer of science-y sounding words, made-up statistics, and anecdotes that may or may not be true. People want to blame someone, and the path of least resistance is blaming some kind of conspiracy by the CDC despite all the actual evidence. It's easier than accepting that bad things just happen.

Being angry at the bogey-man also gives an outlet for anger you might have at yourself, or resentment you might have for your child, way deep down. (#realtalk.) And one last word on this to think about: when you are saying, out loud, that you would rather risk exposing your child and community to a preventable disease that can kill or permanently damage the very young, the very old, the infirm, the immuno-compromised than have an autistic child... as in "Well I still wouldn't risk it! I don't want my kid to get autism just in case!" You are saying you are choosing that over having a child like mine. And honest to God, if you've met my son, who wouldn't want a kid like him?

For a full-on deep dive into the history of Autism, go read <u>In a Different Key</u> by John Donvan and Caren Zucker.

WHAT IS AUTISM SPECTRUM DISORDER?

ASD is at its heart a formula: sensory issues, communication issues, and the "auto" part from which the disorder derives its name, an extreme self-focus which can manifest many ways. These elements can manifest in numerous ways and in varying degrees, hence the "spectrum." For my son, he would hyperfocus on things, namely Star Wars and Minecraft and couldn't/wouldn't talk about much else.

Two terms that are useful to know here: echolalia and scripting. Echolalia is communicating by reciting lines from tv or movies. One time E asked me to play with him but was upset when I wasn't saying the right lines as the character he had assigned to me. Scripting is a fairly similar concept: it's the memorization of things to say. Both of these manifest in repetition, to the point where you might think, "Can't this kid talk about anything else?" And for the ASD child the answer is literally "No." For E, this has improved with therapy but is still there in the undercurrent of his thoughts.

SENSORY OVERLOAD

My son is uncomfortable in social situations and may seem like he's not listening, but he literally may not even know you are talking to him. In the sensory area, he basically hears all noises at once and can't filter them out. He gets overwhelmed in the classroom, noisy restaurants, any place where multiple people are talking or there are loud noises. He doesn't like darkness. He doesn't like things touching the palm of his hand. He can't tolerate certain textures in food. And this is the "high-functioning" end. Other kids on the spectrum literally can't touch certain things, for example sand, because it's painful. Some can't speak at all. Some react in violence when overwhelmed, where E will shut down or get upset in a different way. There are different triggers for different kids. There is one common denominator though- the autistic person literally can't help it.

You may never know how hard a parent is working to help their kid manage. My personal philosophy and faith tell me certain behaviors are not acceptable, but the approach is different. My perspective is training vs. discipline. E doesn't do certain things out of disobedience or disrespect, like not responding when an adult talks to him. But that doesn't mean I let him just not respond. I prompt him to answer because he needs to, but I don't come down hard on him because he isn't at fault. In all this, I will say one of the hardest things for me was realizing that pre-diagnosis I had been treating things as discipline issues that weren't. Realizing you've been treating your child this way, as if they had a choice and were making the wrong one, is devastating.

With that being said, implying in any way to the parent of an autistic kid that if they'd just parent better their kid would be fine is ignorant and annoying at best, and deeply offensive at worst. I'm not a big fan of telling people what to say/what not to say, but I will offer this: if you aren't opening your mouth to tell a weary mom or dad that they are an actual rock star, close it, walk away, and do some self-reflecting. I have been blessed beyond measure to have the most understanding, loving, supporting group of friends an autism mom could ask for though, so that is a theoretical piece of advice.

I KNOW WHAT YOU CAN DO WITH YOUR ESSENTIAL OILS

When people hear about a diagnosis like this, I think they panic. People want to say something, and sometimes say the wrong thing. I am mostly okay with this. Who among us hasn't been super awkward at one point or another? It's nice to have people acknowledge your struggle, and I don't believe that you have to have experienced 100% of the same struggle to relate to someone. We've all had dreams be derailed, or suffered in some way, and therein lies the common ground. There are some questions I don't know how to respond to, since autism isn't curable. So when people ask me if he's better, like he had a cold or something, I (because I'm a sinner) sometimes want to say, "Still autistic!" But I don't because I'm not a jackass, but also because I know the askers are well-intentioned. They want to enter into our lives and our struggle and I am so grateful for that.

There are things that you just shouldn't say, though. One of those things is "Well I don't see anything wrong with him!" The deuce you say... unless you have a Ph.D. or are a licensed therapist, actually even if you are... never say this. Ever. Ok? One time an awesome friend of mine at church said to me, "He seems fine at church, but then, I'm not at home with you all." This was so perfect. It was encouraging about how his behavior at church isn't noticeably off, but acknowledging that she doesn't know what our day to day life is like. Saying something like "What? He seems fine to me!" is so invalidating. My fight for a diagnosis when I knew something was wrong was comparatively easy to other stories I've heard. Skeptical family, skeptical friends, know-it-all, unhelpful people in the medical field... this is all relatively new to being widely accepted so it is hard to identify, accept, and move forward with looking for answers. To be treated like you must be making it up or you're taking things too seriously or if you'd just parent better it would be fine feels like garbage. Even if you think you're being encouraging by saying that, take it from me, you are not.

Another aspect that is terrifying of sharing an autism diagnosis is you never know who's going to try to come at you with anti-vax propaganda. I don't care what you read on Natural News; there is no proven link between vaccines and autism. But somehow, because Oprah and Jenna McCarthy say so, we have people who are convinced vaccines are poison. But that is not why you don't go after someone who just got a diagnosis with your anti-vax crusade. No one asked you. You aren't being brave. You aren't just being an educator. You aren't doing that person a favor. You are telling them that it is their fault that their child has this neurological problem. You are telling them that they did this to their child. You are laying more guilt and blame and shame. So don't tell yourself you're a hero if you do this.

Another poor response is trying to sell someone a cure. If you are in direct sales, more power to you! I used to be to! But if you hear of someone's diagnosis, whether it be autism, ADHD, anxiety, or whatever, and your first response is to try to sell that person something that will help, please stay in your lane. If that person approaches you and wants to talk, great. DO NOT bring it up first. This especially applies if you are into essential oils. Please don't try to tell me that rubbing thieves' oil on my son will magically put his brain back in order. It won't.

You are not a neurologist, psychologist, psychiatrist, or licensed therapist. You are dispensing stupid and quite possibly dangerous advice to vulnerable people. I have had a couple people talk to me about oils but in a really great way… they know people that have tried using them for similar situations and wanted to know if I wanted to get in touch with that other person. That is helpful. It is not someone trying to sell me something as a response to my pain or dispense unqualified advice.

THEOLOGY OF AUTISM

The word "disorder" is so interesting to me on many levels. When God made the world, it was made with order. The Genesis account, whatever perspective you take on it (literal, framework, etc,) exhibits a major theme of harmony. Everything works together perfectly, from the literary details of how the account is told and the parallelism within what is created on each day, to how it all worked physically. Adam and Eve were at peace with themselves, each other, the land, and the animals, and then sin happened.

Everything was disordered. Adam and Eve were barred from the Garden and nothing worked like it was originally supposed to anymore. And the whole story of the Gospel is putting the pieces back together. The salvific work of Christ on the cross redeems all of creation. It is about our eternal souls, but also about the redemption that can take place in the here and now.

In the Reformed tradition, there is a theological shorthand phrase, "the now and the not yet." This refers to the manifestations of redemption we get here: the assurance of salvation, the temporal experiences we have of worship, the peace in our souls, and the manifestations we will receive when Christ comes back: ultimate perfection, perfect harmony with Christ after a lifetime of knowing the pieces don't all quite fit like they're supposed to. And sometimes, my tradition makes this too focused on the spiritual. The work of redemption is also physical. You see this when Jesus raises Lazarus from the dead.

Jesus tells Martha in John 11 that her brother will rise again. She responds in faith that she knows he will, at the final resurrection. Jesus's response is one of the most famous verses in the Gospels: "I am the resurrection and the life. Whoever believes in Me, though he die, yet he shall live, and everyone who lives and believes in me shall never die. Do you believe this?" It's a question for all of us; do we believe this?

Martha does and Jesus gives a beautiful picture of redemption in the physical world. He brings Lazarus back to life. Death is not a thing that was ever supposed to happen. It is a disharmonious piece of life on earth now, and Jesus, who could have just affirmed her earlier statement of belief, of looking forward to the final resurrection and reunion with her brother, gave them a glimpse of what completed restoration will look like. It's spiritual and physical. God cares about our minds, hearts, and bodies.

My son's therapists are in the business of re-ordering my son's disordered brain- and that's really what it is. His brain doesn't know how to sort information, or sometimes holds on in a way that is abnormal.

It's out of order in the literal sense, while ironically demanding order of his world to the point that it sometimes interferes with his enjoyment of it.

PERSPECTIVE

Many years ago at an eye doctor appointment, I was diagnosed with astigmatism. I found out that this problem is what made me see lights the way I do- as a starburst pattern. Street lights, headlights on a car, even Christmas lights- they appear fractured to me, and not as beams. I had no idea this wasn't normal. Funnily enough, I loved looking at lights! Driving down the road at night and seeing these beautiful bursts of pieces of light filled me with joy. Finding out this was not actually how I'm supposed to be experiencing light didn't change much. It was so like God to give me beauty in the brokenness. My vision was distorted and I didn't even know it. I don't know what it is like to look at the world from the fragmented perspective of autism and ADHD but I do know that God gives beauty from ashes (Isaiah 61.)

In the summer of 2018, shortly after we received the autism diagnosis and shortly before school started, I sat in a seminar on the 8 ways children are smart, as taught by the incomparable Dr. Kathy Koch. She described the characteristics of a particular kind of smart, and they included introspection, needing to be alone to process, thinking long and deeply about issues, and as she was talking, it sounded like she was describing my child. Then she mentioned that autistic children have this kind of "smart." I had not thought about the tendencies my son displays because of his autism as a strength, so this was a much-needed paradigm shift for me. He is a deep thinker, a lover of justice, a reflective and gentle soul, and it is because he is autistic that he has these amazing qualities.

A passage that I often reflect on is Romans 8:18-25: "For I consider that the sufferings of this present time are not worthy to be compared with the glory that is to be revealed to us. For the anxious longing of the creation waits eagerly for the revealing of the sons of God. For the creation was subjected to futility, not willingly, but because of Him who subjected it, in hope that the creation itself also will be set free from its slavery to corruption into the freedom of the glory of the children of God. For we know that the whole creation groans and suffers the pains of childbirth together until now. And not only this, but also we ourselves, having the first fruits of the Spirit, even we ourselves groan within ourselves, waiting eagerly for *our* adoption as sons, the redemption of our body. For in this hope we have been saved, but hope that is seen is not hope; for who hopes for what he *already* sees? But if we hope for what we do not see, with perseverance we wait eagerly for it."

My son has this range of disorders because the world is broken. Nature is broken. Everything longs for restoration, and our daily struggles remind me of this keenly. Ultimately we have the redemption of our bodies to look forward to. I have hope that moves me forward every day, as the therapists give us help and something else clicks and I have new strategies to help my son function, and this is just a little reflection of the great hope we have. Perseverance and waiting characterize this journey. I didn't do anything wrong that gave my son autism; it's just a product of the curse in Genesis 3.

Viewing training my child through this lens presents its own challenge within the Christian community. I personally don't come across this often, but I know the attitude is out there that with the right kind of discipline, or if I just parent harder, everything will be fine. That just isn't true. But, I believe that there are qualities we are called to as Christians that my son doesn't get a pass from just because it's harder for him. The fruit of the spirit come to mind: love, joy, peace, patience, kindness, goodness, gentleness, self-control. Some of these are hard for him because of the disruption in his brain due to the disorders. He has anxiety. Peace is hard to come by. But through therapy and medication, it is improved.

We talk about praying and casting our cares on Christ when we worry, but as shocking as this may sound, that doesn't cure his anxiety. It will never cure his anxiety. God gave us amazing medical technology and advances to help in this battle of taking responsibility for our actions... so he takes his pills and we give God the glory.

My son loves deeply though most people wouldn't know it because he's not expressive about his feelings in a typical way. He doesn't hug or say "I love you" voluntarily to anyone but his siblings. The only people allowed in his personal space are his best friend and little brother. His way of showing love is sharing information. If he trusts you, he will want to tell you things. I always know how excited he is about something depending on the number of his old teachers he wants to tell. When I've been gone and he misses me, his way of showing me that is by showing me something new he learned on Minecraft.

Self-control? There are behaviors that are harder for him to rein in. If his brain is on overload, his body responds in a way that he literally has no control over. For us, self-control comes in the ability to recognize and head off a meltdown before it happens. If things go too far and I am telling him "Hey, stop doing that!" I might as well be telling him, "Hey, stop being autistic!" because it will avail the same result: nothing. Our strategies by necessity look very different. Fortunately for some situations, he has a very black and white view of the world so if he is given rules he will follow them to the death. He also really wants to please and gets upset if he thinks he's not doing that, which can cause quite the cycle in a kid who literally can't read a room. But he can learn.

HIDE IT IN YOUR HEART

One strategy I've taken, since I don't have a Christian therapist to follow me around and tell me "That's disorder, that's cuz he's 8, that is definitely a discipline issue!" is to have E memorize scripture. That kid can MEMORIZE. So I put scripture in his mind. I believe that God gave us a spirit not of fear but of power and love and self-control (2 Timothy 1:7) and that the word of God is living and active (Hebrews 4:12). If his brain is going to hold on to and file away everything he reads, then I want God's words permeating his mind and creating the framework by which he views the world.

A problem in the Church is that it's easy to be accidentally dismissive of other people's pain by quoting Bible verses at them. Reminding grieving, reeling parents that God perfectly ordained the situation is in fact theologically accurate, but pretty irritating depending on the timing and the messenger. It is true that God doesn't make mistakes, and my son was fearfully and wonderfully made, and I believe that. But that doesn't make everything ok. It does make me feel like somehow I shouldn't grieve or that you think I just need more faith and everything would be hunky-dory. There's a time and a place. But God promises in His word that all things work together for His glory, even this, even when we can't see the full scope, and may never see it.

I can look back on parts of life and see how the seemingly disparate parts have prepared me for now. I have a Master's degree in theology but I taught English for basically my entire adult life. My first year teaching, with no qualifications and no experience, I worked at a community-model school for special needs kids. I sometimes have flashbacks to how those families operated. Some of them I'm still in touch with. I had no idea at the time I'd be in the ranks. My theology degree has prepared me for the crazy questions my son asks me. He will read something in his Bible, or hear something at church, and ponder, ponder, ponder, until he's formulated his questions. He asked me in line at Disney once if God knew that Adam and Eve would eat of the tree of the knowledge of good and evil, why was He heartbroken over it? Some other questions have been, why are angels and humans different? Is it ok to hate Satan? Is Adam older than Jesus?

A parenting dilemma I have is his black and white, OCD nature. The categories he puts things in don't leave much room for grace, in my opinion, and though he is a professsing Christian, I am left wondering how much is in his heart, and how much of it is that he sees it as a right category? But God's grace upon grace (John 1:16) can will and work whatever and however it wants. His faith may never look like mine but that doesn't mean it's

JESSICA EGGLESTON

not real.

COMPARISON IS THE THIEF OF JOY

That's an oft quoted saying but I have a confession. It's impossible not to compare. I compare my children to each other. I compare them to other people's children. When you're raising your firstborn, there's no baseline. If you are on your second or third (or more) child, you get a sense just because of experience of what's normal and what's not, if your household is fairly conventional. You don't have that with your first.

When I get Timehop videos (flashbacks on social media) of my son talking when he was 3 and 4, every single time I ask myself how we didn't know there was a problem and get him help. His speech his hard to understand, unmodulated, and sometimes slurred together. But at the time I understood him clearly. My daughter is advanced in areas my son was behind in, which makes the contrast stand out all the more. Her verbal ability at 2 was more clear than his at 4. Her fine motor control and outward artistic creativity is beyond his. Her emotional IQ, communication skills, and confidence are all way beyond. But he excels at things she didn't.

At age 4 she couldn't read yet, where he was

reading way beyond his age level by then. I have no idea what's normal because I have yet to experience it. The blessing there is that they played well together because of their naturally complementing personalities and similar interests, where my daughter's advancements and E's deficits overlap. At the time of publishing, my son is in middle school and that's a whole new ball game.

In the age of social media it is not possible to stay away from comparison. I often want to yell at people who complain about being busy because they've filled up their schedule voluntarily. Drive across town for multiple therapy appointments a week on different days, take care of the homework for therapy, home-school 2 very different children, then have a third child who was born with a physical deformity and then come talk to me about busy. (I have to point out here, I don't think my busy-ness makes me better. It did, however, give me an anxiety disorder!)

Then there's the level of achievement. Part of what set off red flags for us was noticing the social differences between our son and his classmates, so in some ways that was a good thing, though difficult, but it is a constant reminder of the future that doesn't exist when I see people posting about their kid's success in sports or feeding the homeless or whatever.

This one is a hard one. Comparison is needed in some degree because that is how you know if something is wrong or how much progress is being made. Benchmarks exist for a reason, and this is why it is important to have professional help. They will be professionally detached in looking at how the numbers and evaluations match up and set goals for where your child needs to be. This is much more effective and productive than fretting over what you observe yourself in other people's kids. Once you've done that, you need to, in some degree, put blinders on and worry about what progress looks like for your child, and let the professionals work on what your child's progress looks like on their age-appropriate scale.

Comparison when you have more than one child is basically inevitable, in my situation because my neurotypical child's areas of giftedness throw into sharp relief the struggles of her older brother.

CELEBRATE AVERAGE

It's somewhat ironic that I'm a schoolteacher because now I'm in a position where I see vividly how unfair it can be to celebrate high academic achievement solely by recognizing perfect scores. If prizes were given for having to work hard to get what you have, we'd be cleaning up. But the classroom doesn't operate that way, and neither do our lives. In therapyland, the goal is average. If you're in therapy, it's because your skillset is poor. Statistically you are far below the other people your age. You get dismissed from therapy when you reach average, not excellent. The bar is "acceptable enough to not need therapy services on the reg." Every time we've been graduated from therapy (I'm using that term because it sounds so much nicer than "dismissed!" I've been both glad but also filled with terror. Every parent wants the best for their kid. I have had to come to terms with the best looking very, very different.

FEELING BAD THAT YOU FEEL BAD BECAUSE OTHERS HAVE IT WORSE

This is another thing in the category of what not to say to someone who just found out a diagnosis. There is a time for giving perspective, and only if you have a privileged role in that person's life. Telling someone who is grieving that other people have it worse so they shouldn't feel bad is not a helpful thing to say. Trust me, we do this well enough on our own.

There is a vicious cycle that starts in your head that goes something like this: "Man I wish this wasn't my life. But I know other people have it worse. I shouldn't feel bad. But I feel bad. Now I feel worse because I know other people have it worse and here I am complaining." For you to pile on that just makes everything worse. I don't need to be told that others have it worse. I'm well aware. If you are my best friend and you know I'm sliding into self-pity, a gentle reminder might be necessary, but if that's not your role, don't talk.

If you're a Christian, think of what you're supposed to do biblically and carry one another's burdens. Let that person know you don't understand what they're going through but you'd like to understand, or offer some encouragement. That is always welcome! ALL moms feels this way, much less special needs moms, I'm pretty sure. You have a hard day, you're stressed, you wonder why it has to be this way, and then you see or hear someone else's story that is no question harder than yours. (Or at least it seems that way.) Then the cycle starts because you weren't grateful for your blessings, and at least you don't have it worse, and you shouldn't ever let yourself have bad feelings and definitely never speak them out loud because you should just feel hashtag blessed at all times.

Y'all. CUT THAT MESS OUT.

Some people have it better than you. Some have it worse. Sometimes you just don't know the whole story and it's not your business anyway. It is ok to recognize when something is hard. There is definite tension between recognizing something is a problem in order to deal with it, and recognizing something is a problem so you can wallow around in it for whatever reason. But it is just as unhealthy to live in guilt that you dared to be sad because your kid can't do normal kid stuff as it is to be constantly self-pitying.

You can't help your child unless you are honest

with the problem and give it a name, and you can't help yourself, or be helped by others, if you don't give honest voice to your feelings. Find a trusted person to talk to that can help you find the balance. Perspective is always good, counting your blessings is always good, but grief and disappointment aren't unholy feelings. Let it wash over you, then deal with it.

COMMUNITY WARS

I had no idea about the disagreement between autism groups when I first started down this road, but in brief, there are opposing camps: one that wants to find a cure, and one that thinks there's nothing to cure, and the very suggestion of such is a dehumanizing insult. I think this issue is much more complex than that. If my son was on the extreme end, I'm sure I'd be in the "find a cure" camp with more emotional investment. I am a big proponent of early intervention and therapy because of my experience and what I've seen in others. It's the closest thing to a "cure" that exists right now: teaching kids with difficulties interacting socially because of autism how to function in the world.

In a perfect world, everyone would be perfectly loving and accepting and accommodating but that is not the case. I would not be doing my son any favors for his future life by pretending that everyone will be understanding of him. I want him to be independent, have a fulfilling career, have a family... if I hid from reality, hid from help and indulged his disabilities I believe I'd be ruining his life. But, I also think that there are many facets of this process that could benefit everyone. The things that he needs to learn are so valuable for everyone. Who couldn't benefit from learning empathy and conversation skills?

In one of his therapies, because autism kids by definition are self-focused, we practice thinking of others. It becomes a discipline. Asking other people about themselves is the same way. We practice questions, making observations, pretending at being interested until it becomes real. I think everyone could stand to take a class in how to think of others more! It's not treating my son as less-than to get him the help he needs, and I think that is the major philosophical flaw behind the "don't try to fix me" camp. There are many rich and fulfilling things in his life brought about exactly because of his disorders that help me be a better person. I have had to reevaluate my own ideas of what success are.

As a professional educator, I became more enlightened to what might be going on behind certain classroom behaviors that were disruptive/annoying. I learned a new word: neurotypical. I'm not trying to make my son be that, because he just isn't, but I'd like him to not unnecessarily struggle. The camp that wants a cure don't want their children struggling either, and when they look for a cure, they look for something that will make their kids speak, stop injuring themselves, stop running away... because they love their children and would do anything for them, not because they view their child as sub-human. I think both camps could learn from each other.

I think a key is how parents speak about and treat their children. It's just an undeniable truth that having a special needs child makes your life harder. It's ok to speak that out loud. It doesn't mean you don't love your child. It makes you realize what love really is in many ways: giving up your own vision for the future, to build a future for your child. Sacrificing time, money, energy, that could have gone to anything else in order to get your child into therapy services. Realizing that there is beauty in neurodiversity.

"THE IMAGE OF GOD IS NOT LINKED TO POTENTIALITY"

I wrote that quote down listening to a lecture from Dr. Grant Macaskill, a professor of the University of Aberdeen. Another time, I heard an autism mom and expert decry the idea that people have of valuing life based on accomplishment, in the context of asking why someone would bother fighting so hard for their autistic child when they won't become a brain surgeon. Both are just a different way of expressing the same idea: that life is valuable because it's life. We have a tendency in modern America to conflate inherent value with a quantifiable idea of worth/profit. The value of life is immeasurable because it is implicit in humanity, and when you try to make it anything else it leads down dangerous paths.

Arguing the right to live because a person could possibly become a productive member of society plays into that view. We need to reclaim, loudly, boldly, that life is valuable simply because it is life. Related to that idea is the concept we have of normal, that we then measure people against. Who got to decide that anyway? But we do have recognizable, deep-seated "norms" that we want to force people into. But what is normal?

In biblical terms, I believe autism is just as normal as our sin nature. Our sin nature traps us into patterns the way autism traps the autistic person into patterns. It's constitutional, not external. Until we're set free from sin by the power of the Holy Spirit, we often don't even recognize that we were trapped in that pattern. Likewise, an autistic person doesn't necessarily know they're trapped into a pattern, and if they do know, they don't know how to get out of it. Both require an external work to solve this intrinsic problem.

Transformation starts on the outside, sinking in and working inside to out as external practices start to sink in to the heart, soul, and mind. In therapy, brain function can literally be changed because of physical practices, the same way that holiness is a practice. It's not the natural inclination. My son has to be taught empathy, how to listen, converse, notice others, and pick up on social cues. But the things he has to learn how to do, we are instructed to do in the Bible. Neurotypical people may have these same struggles. Why else would God tell us to abide by the Fruit of the Spirit? (Love, joy, peace, patience, kindness, goodness, gentleness, and self-control?) Those don't come naturally to anybody; some just fake it better.

THE LEAST OF THESE

Matthew 25 speaks of judgment based on your treatment of the least of these. Jesus says how you treat them, or don't treat them, you are doing to Him. If you dismiss someone's worth because you think they can't contribute anything, you are dismissing Jesus. (Plus, you're severely deluded.)

OVERLY LITERAL AND OTHER STRUGGLES

There was this one time before school I told my son to go get his water bottle. What I meant was "Go get your water bottle, fill it up, and put it in your backpack for school like we do every day." But that isn't what I said. I said "Go get your water bottle." So he got his water bottle, put it on the kitchen counter, empty, and went back to whatever it was he was doing before we had to leave. In that moment, and so many others like it, I had to stop myself from getting frustrated with him because I know better. I know he doesn't understand subtlety or implication. I need to be very clear about what I mean. In the classroom, this can cause difficulties.

Often times we get along in social situations by picking up on invisible clues. What is everyone else doing? What are their facial expressions? What is the mood in the room? My son doesn't pick up on these things. Maybe he never will but we're working on it. In class when everyone else knows it's time to work on math so they get their books out and start working, even kids who maybe missed the verbal cueing will notice what their tablemates are doing and get their work out. Not my kid! He needed to be told specifically what to do, until he caught on to the routine and then it's cemented in his brain forever. (Until the routine changed and then it's back to square 1.) He could look at his classmates with their math books and notebooks and pencils and it WOULD NOT OCCUR TO HIM that he ought to do the same thing. Combined with the fact that he writes slowly and messily, and processes slowly, it gives him a major disadvantage in the classroom. Anything based on speed is inherently unfair to him. He can do incredibly complicated math in his head and talk it out but the traditional classroom setting is set up in direct opposition to his ability to show what he knows. Much of this has gotten better since the beginning, but this will always be an issue.

At home, this is also a struggle. I am all about non-literal thinking. I'm an extrovert. My son needs to memorize idioms so he can understand what people are talking about. If he has been around people too much, fun or not, he's in danger of a meltdown. One strategy we have in place to help him is that we require quiet rest time. This used to be on a daily basis, but now we work on a more as-needed basis. We explained to E that he needed the time by himself to recover, and he recognizes more and more in himself when he needs to separate himself. We go to a very small church, and we share the space with another church that overlaps in time, so the places we can go on the property are limited. Before and after church, many of the kids will race back and forth in the foyer and it gets very loud. A major sign of progress is that many times now instead of getting to the point of no return, E will come sit by himself in the sanctuary and just be.

Another difficulty he has is in moving from parts to the whole (forming/recognizing a gestalt, to use the technical term.) This reflects in his standardized testing scores, among other things. One year he scored above the national average in every single breakdown of every single category in academics. But on the test that measured critical thinking and application, the scores dropped. This is the same result that occurs on every test he gets at every doctor and therapy office, which is both encouraging that every expert is seeing the same thing but also frustrating because the pieces are all there, it's just hard to put together.

Putting things in context is a struggle we have. E will often start talking to me without getting my attention and get upset when I ask him to start over, or change topics midstream without warning so that I again don't know what he's talking about, or will launch into a story or question about something he was thinking about, without giving me the background information. One of his therapists explained to me that he is great about expressing what is important to him. The rest of it is there, he just has to learn how to explain it. He is also very visual in that he can picture exactly what it is he means but there is a massive breakdown in communication when he has to try to explain something verbally.

E gets really frustrated if I don't understand him right away, partly because in his head he's being perfectly clear and doesn't understand why I don't understand, but also I suspect he feels unvalued which is not true, but also not something he could express to me. It's just my mom's intuition. I have to try to calmly explain that I want to listen and understand but he has to let me know he's talking to me, and explain what he is talking about so that I can understand it. This is actually another skill he worked on with his speech therapist. They played a game of describing objects to the other person until they can understand. E is working on giving the right kind of details to get the other person to know what he's talking about.

SENSORY 101

There are many behaviors that manifest in autistic kids that are related to sensory processing. Sensory processing disorder can be its own diagnosis, but in the case of my child it was a symptom of being on the spectrum. He still doesn't like things touching the palm of his hand. He has an overwhelming, often compulsive need to chew on things. There's just something very satisfying to him about doing that. Tags in his shirts are a huge distraction. Any food that is too slimy is a no-go; he will literally throw up so I know it's not just a picky kid thing. This can cause for some awkward situations.

I knew the texture-food issue was the real deal when we were visiting my aunt and uncle in their home state a couple years ago. My aunt is a wonderful cook and had made a delicious breakfast casserole, which we were all enjoying when all of a sudden E gagged it out onto his plate. There were tiny pieces of cooked mushroom in the casserole. And I mean, so tiny I didn't even know they were there and I LOVE mushrooms. E didn't know either; it was just his body's response to the texture of that particular food. Everyone felt bad for all the reasons I'm sure you can imagine. At this point I've learned he can't eat almost all cooked vegetables. If it remains crunchy, like roasted broccoli or sautéed Brussels sprouts, he's good.

Soft-cooked carrots? Nope.

Sauteed peppers and onions? Extra nope.

Okra? H*** no!

But he will eat almost any vegetable raw, which is great. I've had to learn to make the texture issue and need to chew work for us. He will chow down on crunchy celery, raw peppers, and anything with a pit. I can give him a bowl full of Castelveltrano Italian whole olives and he will eat all of them.

GRIEF

There is grief involved in getting a diagnosis. It is normal and it is ok! Accept and deal with the feelings. The classic stages of Kubler Ross are helpful to think through. (Denial, anger, bargaining, depression, acceptance.)

Denial is a hard one to work through. When you first realize there might be something wrong with your child, or other people in your child's life try to bring it your attention, whether it be a teacher, school counselor, pediatrician, or other person, you probably won't want to believe it. Even if you really truly see it, it's hard to accept. Don't get stuck here!

If a trusted authority in your child's life is trying to help you see there's a problem, I am begging you to listen. It's hard. You don't want to hear it or believe that there is something wrong. But this is the door to getting help and setting up your child for success. It is important to realize that you are in the stages of grief so you can move through them. In many ways, the life you crafted in your head for your child to have is most likely over. Recognize that. Cry for it. Then get moving!

Anger is the next stage, which often goes hand in hand with denial. How did this go wrong? Why my kid? I did everything right! While I wouldn't classify my response as angry, I sometimes get jealous at other people's normalcy. According to grief.com, "The anger is just another indication of the intensity of your love." Of course you're angry! It's not fair! This is your child, for whom you would do anything! I would just advise, try not to lash out at the people trying to tell you your child needs help. It is easy to view those trying to help as criticizing your parenting or somehow blaming you. Trust me; you can't parent a child into or out of autism. It's just a crappy thing that happens to some people. Don't shove the feelings though or they will come pouring out at the worst times!

Bargaining is the next classic stage. (God, if you just do this for me, I'll do/never do this!) This stage manifests, I believe, more in self-blame or trying to find some magic cure. You might think if only I had given him better food, or less screen time, or more socialization, or taken him in earlier... this ends nowhere good. You didn't cause this. And if you're getting help now, congratulate yourself on being a great parent!

It is also easy to start believing every anecdote-based "cure." I don't care if your sister-in-law's neighbor's friend cured their mailman's son's autism with essential oils. Please get involved with actual experts who have studied the physiology, neurology, and therapy treatments that have decades of scientific information to back them up. Don't think if you just do x,y,z (which all just translates to "if I can just be a better parent, the universe/God has to fix him!) Just, no. It doesn't work like that. Don't do that to yourself.

Then comes depression. This is different from the intense roller coaster you may have felt at first because it's more of a settled sadness. Sadness at recognizing your child's struggles, recognizing your own struggles, adjusting to your new doctor/therapy/IEP meeting etc. schedule. It is a lot to deal with and it will seep in to every part of your being if you let it. Get help. Find other parents with the same experiences, whether in person or online. If you don't have a local support group, start one!

The last step is acceptance. This does not mean everything is great and you never feel sad again. It just means you've come to terms with your new normal.

ACCOMMODA-TIONS

My school is a little different. It's a hybrid model private school, where my kids are homeschooled 2 days out of the week. I am closely involved with the teachers as a partner in the education of my children, so accommodations affect all of us. Because it is a private school, it offers "reasonable accommodations" on a case by case basis. (You might have an IEP program. Whatever it is, find out what the procedure is and study it like it's your job.)

In the classroom this might include preferential seating, leaving the classroom for tests so he's not distracted by noisy classmates, and other very simple adjustments to help him not be at a disadvantage. At home it has much more to do with the workload. I have a lot more leeway than I actually took with his work, especially in younger grades. It helps that I taught where he attends, so I'm able to make educated decisions knowing the full scope and sequence of the curriculum throughout all the grades. If I know a particular exercise is going to be repeated many more times, I'm more likely to apply my school-approved license to tinker with assignments than if it's a really focused scaffolding of a skill that he will need for future grades. (Sorry for the jargon.) If that made your eyes glaze over, just think of it this way: what is a necessary future skill? What isn't? Adjustments can be made accordingly.

I was still more likely than not to make him just do everything the way it was assigned in the lesson plans unless the day is just really off the rails. I am very opposed to infantilizing my child by making him think it's ok to not do things, hard as they may be, just because it's challenging. If I never make him struggle through writing, he will never learn what is on the other side of the struggle. I also know that eventually, he will be on his own, living his life, and needing to be independent.

I'm not going to hold his hand through college and beyond, and teaching him to advocate for himself, work through the struggle, and honestly do his best, starts now. I also have realistic expectations of the world. Sometimes people are kind; sometimes they are cruel. Most often they are ambivalent, as long as you're doing your job or whatever. My world revolves around my kids, but no one else's does. When he's out on his own doing whatever career work he wants to do, I don't expect anyone to require less of him because he has some disorders.

There are plenty of things that make my son special but he doesn't need to ever feel entitled, and I've seen that every so often in my years teaching. I have also seen incredible models of families that have handled similar issues SO well, training their kids to be self-advocates, not be afraid to ask for help, but not be afraid to reach for goals they've been told they can't reach. It's a constant tight-rope of thinking what will help most in the moment, the day, the week, and down the road, and what am I sacrificing in the meantime. I could make things easier for him but I don't always believe that's the right way.

Now here's the deal. I know my kid, I know his capabilities, I'm in constant conversation with his therapists, teachers, the academic director of our school, and I'm a teacher. I'm in a position a lot of people aren't necessarily in when it comes to this kind of stuff. That doesn't mean you can't successfully advocate for your child. My best tip: be kind but firm. Get to know all the people who make those decisions for your student. But know that no one is going to fight for your child like you will.

JUST DO IT

One time I was getting ready to go out for a date night with my husband when I heard my daughter screaming. I ran to find her, and somehow, she had gotten a jar of cayenne pepper, opened it, and rubbed it all over her face and into her eyes. I grabbed her and ran into the shower, both of us fully clothed, to wash it off as fast as I could. It was a wrestling match to hold my writhing, screaming, now soaking wet child to spray her in the face until the pepper was gone from her eyes. It wasn't fun. But it was the only option. When your child is in need, you do what you need to do, even if you have to dry off, change clothes, and redo your makeup!

In all my adventures with my oldest, going to therapy and doctor appointments and whatnot, I've had several people marvel at how quickly I acted from the very first recommendation of his teacher to take him to an occupational therapist til now. While I love attention and getting compliments, I don't think this is something really laudable in me. If your teacher or other expert thinks your child needs help, you drop everything and help them. This ought to be normal.

I share about our experience because I want others

to see how much help we've had. I am able to identify my son's needs and adjust my parenting to his capabilities. I'm far from perfect and there are some days I get really, really exasperated with him. But with things like SPD, autism, adhd, anxiety, and everything else he has going on... I can't muddle through that alone. He won't grow out of it, even though the progress he has made is unbelievable. You can't discipline it out. I know there are a variety of reasons people have for not taking their kid to a medical professional... being afraid of labels or of medication... but there are so many resources out there.

Don't be afraid of the labels. Labels get you answers. Labels get you help. Labels get you in doors to people you otherwise would never have known you needed. Accept it and embrace it.

I've been blessed with professionals who have gotten to know my son and gotten to know me, my parenting philosophy, how I feel about medication, and on and on. But I have full realization that I am not a therapist, psychologist, or pediatric behavioral expert. I can educate myself but an article I find on the internet does not have equal weight with someone who has made this their life's work. So, if you're reading this, and you have been told by people who know that your child might need help, what are you waiting for?